Pigs Might Fly

JOHN HEATH-STUBBS was born in 1918 and educated at Queen's College, Oxford. A critic, anthologist and translator as well as a poet, he has received the Queen's Gold Medal for Poetry and the prestigious St Augustine Cross. In 1988 he was awarded the OBE.

Also by John Heath-Stubbs from Carcanet

The Watchman's Flute
Naming the Beasts
The Immolation of Aleph
Collected Poems
Selected Poems
Literary Essays (edited by Trevor Tolley)
Sweetapple Earth
Galileo's Salad
The Sound of Light
The Return of the Cranes

As editor
Thomas Gray, *Selected Poems*

JOHN HEATH-STUBBS

Pigs Might Fly

CARCANET

First published in Great Britain in 2005 by
Carcanet Press Limited
Alliance House
Cross Street
Manchester M2 7AQ

A CIP catalogue record for this book is available from the British Library
ISBN 1 85754 819 1

The publisher acknowledges financial assistance from Arts Council England

Typeset by XL Publishing Services, Tiverton
Printed and bound in England by SRP Ltd, Exeter

Contents

The Day that Pigs Learned to Fly

It was a warm evening, and the sun not set.
I was in my garden and enjoying it,
When suddenly I noticed something moving in the air,
And a slight musical grunting. I looked up –
What did I see but a big white pig
Floating about in the sky and speaking or singing as well as grunting.
It seemed to hover in the evening air,
And purposefully, when, lo and behold,
The sky was full of *cochons*,
As they soared and swerved and swooped,
Exactly by what means I could not discern.
That was many years ago. I am an old man now,
And the sight's so familiar
That I am told people don't look up now as once they did,
In Trafalgar Square, where folk come in the evening
To find a cinema or a theatre open or to catch a helicopter
To take them back to the suburbs after work,
And observe, above the National Gallery
And St Martin's Church, and the archaic statue of Lord Nelson,
Lots of little piggies fluttering about and squealing.
It's so familiar, it hardly catches their attention,
Though once it was one of the marvellous sights of London,
In the early decades of the Third Millennium.

Cat and Dog

A friend I knew once had, in the war years
Served in Africa, and loved that continent –
The countries, and the people.
He told me once how, when a spotted panther
Found her way into a farm, first thing she'd do
Was slaughter all the dogs that might be there
The old cat and dog feud, he said –
But now the odds were on the cat's side not the dog's –
She'd slaughter every one. We've seen that feud
Whenever a terrier or else a spaniel
Has tree'd a cat, and barks in hatred at her
'Come down milk-sopper, come down to the fighting ground
Mouse-muncher! Sit-by-the-fire and slaughterer
Of scruffy little sparrows!'
The dog remains in dudgeon – he
No way can climb a tree-trunk,
But must retire, frustrated.
His kin, the subtle foxes – they can climb
At least a bit, and best of all,
The little fennec foxes –
Those that spoil the vines.

A Mnemonic

The tortoise lives upon the dry land;
The turtle in the depths of the sea;
The terrapin in rivers and fresh water pools –
So don't you confuse the three.

Penge – Moral Standards Vindicated

A respectable person from Penge
Exacted a frightful revenge
On his unfaithful wife
For he ended her life
On the altar stone at Stonehenge.

The Tadpoles

'I shall be newt,' said the first tadpole,
'Sporting a golden waistcoat.'
'I shall be a toad,' said the second,
'And walk with dignity across the thoroughfare.'
'And I a hopping, skipping frog,' the third,
'And croak difficult operatic arias.'
But a black and white and tufted duck
Plunged into the water and swallowed all three.

Poem Intended to be Inscribed on a Manhole Cover in a London Pavement

Incline your head, passer-by, and peruse what you see
With some danger from passing perambulators
Not to mention incontinent sparrows and pigeons.
Here is a long, thin thing coiling around.
It isn't a centipede, but an unrhymed poem –
Free verse at that! What is it there for –
Only to prove what a cultured place
This town of ours is – evidently?

Pollen

Pollen that blows on the summer breeze,
Like dust, that bears an anonymous love-letter
To the heart of solitary flowers,
Was fossilised, through aeons and aeons of time
From a light powder, to hard and brilliant gem-stones –
Sapphires, emeralds, rubies or chrysoprase –
Into light jewels, yet almost perdurable –
Like these words of mine perhaps, gem-stones
To adorn the mortal bodies
Of men or women – famous beauties,
Decking the crowns of Persian emperors.
The unlettered populace beholding this from a distance
Thought their ruler was shadowed
By the radiance of Ahura Mazda.
Likewise these stones enhanced
Celebrated courtesans –
For diamonds after all, as the song says, is
A girl's best friend.

Cephalopods

Argonaut pilots a paper cradle –
Floating on sunlit seas;
Ammonites evolve, coil and then uncoil;
Octopus relinquishes one arm to find a mate for him,
But she will never know his charms;
In the depths the kraken waits
Until the end of time; cuttle-bone is good
To sharpen a canary's beak.

Fitzroy

You know the name, in connection with gale-warnings and so on.
It used to be Finisterre, but there are too many Lands-Ends it seems;
This Fitzroy was captain of *The Beagle*,
Darwin's friend he was and his companion;
Later an admiral, he did some work
On the frequency of storms off the south-west coast of England.
The captain needed someone to talk to,
For he was a depressive – scion of Lord Castlereagh,
Who'd cut his throat in terror and despair.
The captain's fundamentalist beliefs
Were challenged by all the astonishing discoveries
Darwin made, as by the inhumanity of man to man
In the indigenous savages – but more in their Hispanic rulers.
The Fitzroy family tree originated in the philanderings
Of that notorious gold-digger, Lady Castlemaine,
With her sovereign –
Charles the Second, 'one of the most intelligent
And also the most charming of all our kings'
(So Neville Coghill termed him,
In the first lecture I ever attended at Oxford).
Admiral Fitzroy
Had a tavern named after him,
In what is really part of Bloomsbury but north of Soho.
I guess he installed one of his officers there as its first landlord.
I knew it well in my early London days –
There were a few moral shipwrecks there, no doubt.

Madame Butterfly

I enjoy opera, but there's one work
In the repertoire I really cannot take:
Giacomo Puccini's *Madame Butterfly*.
Perhaps we need a concept-production
Set in California – Cho-Cho San a good-time girl from that state
Her Uncle the Bonze a Methodist preacher
And Captain Ping-Ka-Tong of course
An officer in the Japanese navy.
This would be an inversion of the moral –
'Never trust a Yank' –
Quite unjustifiably applied to this work.
In Second World War days
A man I met once had been a singer
Who'd had a role in one of Puccini's pieces.
He told me how he found Puccini
An utterly charming man to work with.
He had, like some Italians,
An almost Syrian face – remember those late Roman slave estates
Stocked with captives from the Middle East –
Relentless pursuer of young girls and wild fowl
That composer was – innocent garganey,
Gadwall, scorp and teal,
Rather than harmless butterflies.

The Tuatera Speaks

Myself and my ancestors,
We've been on this coral reef
For thousands and thousands of years, while the surrounding seas
Were full of ichthyosaurs and plesiosaurs, flapping and splashing about,
While on the neighbouring continental lands
Were vast primeval forests packed with dinosaurs –
Lizard-footed, beast-footed, or bird-footed,
Vegetarian herbivores, or aggressive carnivores,
All of them evolving, while in the sky,
Bat-winged pterodactyls swooped about and flitted.
I was brought up rather to disapprove
Of all this evolution lark, and do it as little as possible.
'Hatteria' is one of the names I've been known by –
But hatters were mad because of the chemical they used,
Also because they try to keep apace with every shifting fashion.
My family have changed as little as we possibly could
And have done quite nicely out of it –
Thank you very much. Our tight little reef
Presented few challenges, but I shall never
Sing like a bird nor nurse my offspring
With a mammal's tenderness. The kind New Zealand government
Protects us now – so we're all right.

Gadarenes

The first anthology was compiled
By a poet, Meleager of Gadara.
There have been plenty since – in our language
The conscientious Palgrave (at his best
When Tennyson was nudging him – but no authentic John Donne,
No adult William Blake). As for Quiller-Couch –
Open his Oxford Book in the middle –
Everything on the right
Is Nineteenth Century, and half that again
Victorian. So much for the early centuries of English verse –
Elizabethan, Metaphysicals and Augustans.
It would be a crack, hardly worth my making, to say
That anthologists are Gadarene Swine,
Rushing down a steep slope into a quagmire of uncertain taste.
But after all, I've done my stint of anthologising too –
Haven't I?

Migrants

A Russian friend, self-exiled from that country,
Unlikely to return, took to jogging
In Kensington Park, every morning early –
One day he witnessed a flock of swans
High in the autumn sky. I told him
These were wild swans – Whoopers or Bewick's,
On migration southwards, from Russian latitudes.
This seemed to please him. It was as if
When they returned he might entrust a message to them
For friends and relatives he'd left behind,
And, maybe, would not ever see again.

Cat Talk

An Anecdote re-told

'The new tom at number twenty-five,'
Said Malkin the cat to Tybaldina her friend,
As they shared a soup-plate of milk,
'Have you met him yet, and what is he like?'
'Yes – on the tiles last night,' Tibbles replied,
'As it happened, but really, my dear, he's a terrible bore,
A dead loss – all he can talk about,
It would seem, is his operation.'

The Frog and the Scorpion

An Anecdote re-told

On the banks of the Nile, a greenery-yallery frog
Sat and was practising his melodious song –
Not a care in the world – when suddenly
A stranger appeared – a monstrous stranger, a scorpion
With lobster-like claws, and a sting in his tail
Arched over his segmented back.
The scorpion greeted the frog, 'Little brother,
Be so good as to take me on your shoulders,
And ferry me across to the opposite bank
Of this great river.' 'No,' said the frog –
He was wary, 'For you will sting me
When we're halfway over
And then we will both of us sink to the bottom.'
'This doesn't make sense,' the scorpion replied,
'That way, the two of us would drown
So do us this favour.' The frog was persuaded,
And he set forth – a good breaststroke, with strong back-kicks,
The scorpion on top. Halfway across,
The scorpion did sting him. 'This,' said the frog,
'Is against all logic – the rational argument which you set before me.'
'You forget, my friend,' the scorpion answered,
'This is the Middle East.'

Homage to Edgar Rice Burroughs

Part One – The Martian Chronicles

Fleeing from his enemies, in the Colorado desert,
Someone takes refuge in a cave.
It turns out to be filled with noxious gas –
So he passes out, with his eyes fixed
On the red planet rising – wakes up
To find himself in that world, which
In spite of its distance from the sun
Has a more than tropical climate.
Its inhabitants – one lot green and vicious,
Six-limbed if I remember right
The other graceful and beautiful and entirely human –
Except they're oviparous – all of them naked, all of the time.
Our hero has an affair with a princess of Mars,
And the two produce an egg.

Part Two – Tarzan

Tarzan, of course, was an English aristocrat –
And so was Jane, his wife.
Now we're familiar with the real great apes –
Gorillas, chimpanzees, orangs.
Gorillas go hunting small game together,
United by a strong homosexual bond.
Chimps are killed for bush-meat –
And tourists can have a taste of it,
A frisson of near-cannibalism.
In Indonesia, there's the orang-utan –
His home is threatened by illegal logging companies –
Babies are snatched from their mothers,
Who are shot to provide
A cute, almost human pet for rich tourists.
It's a long way from how these primates appear in romantic literature –
Sir Oran Haut-on – a candidate for a rotten borough
In Peacock's *Melincourt*. Sylvan from the isle of Taprobane
In Scott's Byzantine novel *Count Robert of Paris*
Who kills his master, a pagan philosopher

Who's just about to rape the heroine. And after that, of course,
The murderer in the Rue Morgue.

It shall be asked of man as once it was of Cain
'*Homo Sapiens*, what have you done
With *Simia Satyrus* – he who was your brother?'

Brock

When the wind whispered in the willows, the badger
Was the wise mentor to the rat and mole;
To those with a less literary childhood
The badger had a meaningful relationship
With Rupert Bear, in Mary Tourtel's interminable verse epic,
Running in a widely circulated daily newspaper.
Now, the badger is a protected species, to be culled
If suspected of carrying the TB virus.
Somebody in *The Archers* takes the law into his own hands,
Shoots the badger, and is tried.
A whole nation listens with bated breath.
'Things could be worse,' said Brock.
'Out there in China
My cousin the ferret-badger is boiled alive
Merely to furnish an evening meal.'

An Oxford Tortoise

Relaxing, one hot summer afternoon –
(Years ago it was, and one whom I loved
Was there as well, but he's no longer with us)
Upon the lawn of an Oxford college garden,
A tortoise we observed among the grasses –
One, or so I'm credibly informed
That once had been a personal acquaintance
Of John Henry Newman – desultorily wandered
(Quite rapidly, for one of his chelonian kind) –
His intent, it seemed, was just to eat the yellow buttercups
That grew profusely there. He did not care a jot or tittle
For the green blades or their wiry stems.
Buttercups have a pungent taste as I recall
From childhood experiments, and they are slightly toxic.
There ought to be a moral to this story –
But I can't think of one so let it pass.

The Duckatrice of Netley Abbey

A Hampshire Story

The nuns of Netley Abbey kept poultry,
Particularly ducks, which they loved best –
It was Sister Jemima, whose charge they were.
These ducks could be relied on to provide an egg
For each sister's breakfast on high holy days,
Maybe a roast duck for their Christmas dinner.
No web-foot birds were ever cosseted that much – but one day
Came among them – a great hooded serpent
(Not a grass-snake, not a coronella, not an adder)
But something out of India or Africa.
A pilgrim must have chanced to introduce it –
By stealth it seems it slipped into a gum-boot.
From thence escaping, it set about seduction
Of all the convent poultry – notably the ducks,
For he would coil around the eggs they dropped and try to hatch them.
Eventually succeeding
Then emerged a long scaly thing, the ducks' webbed feet.
A duckatrice it was whose piercing stare
Turned flesh and blood to stone – and several sisters suffered
Just that dreadful fate (due to slackness
In prayers and duties they'd forfeited
Their Lord's protection, and were petrified).
The Mother Abbess was appalled at this –
Pilgrims kept away, and benefactors
Withdrew subscriptions. Succour came at length –
Matcham, the gardener, armed himself
With a great looking-glass he had got hold of
(Nobody quite knew how – of course the sisters
Were not permitted mirrors, lest they were tempted
Into the deadly sin of vanity).
Matcham suspended this glass in the hole
Wherein the creature coiled. For the first time
It caught a glimpse of its own ugly mug
And froze to solid stone. The Mother Abbess
After consultation now decided
They had better keep this effigy,
A token of their Saviour's loving kindness.
So it remained there until Thomas Cromwell's lot
Ruled it superstitious, and had it broken up

For cobble-stones. Some still lie there
Upon the Winchester Road beneath the tarmac. It is said
They survive at bends and corners
Fraught with peril, for the skids and crashes
That still occur there down to the time of writing.
That's the end of the story. Quack quack.

I Am a Roman

I

I can't now recall his name, if indeed I knew it.
One would encounter him, from time to time, in the Wheatsheaf,
Or in similar venues, in forties or fifties days.
What he did for a living I do not know, but certainly
His knowledge of Roman history was extensive –
An incident he told of – how once in Italy,
He saw a little girl, and she was playing
On top of a high wall. 'Be careful, little girl,' he said,
'Or you'll fall down.' 'Oh no, I won't fall down, Signor,' she answered,
'I am a Roman.'

II

Another thing he said –
In conversation with Nina Hamnett
Who was complaining about the church:
'They teach children things even I can't understand,
The Trinity, for instance.'
'Don't worry about it, Nina,' he answered,
'Even the Archbishop of Canterbury can't do that.'

Carême and the Marquis de Cussy

'As a good book needs no preface, so a good dinner can do without soup.'
This was the Marquis de Cussy's retort to Carême,
Who, you must know, was Talleyrand's cook,
And organised the entire catering programme
For the congress of Vienna. Carême on his death-bed
Besought the Marquis to abjure his heresy.
I hope they're reconciled now,
In some gourmet's heaven, beyond the Pot-star, far from that inferno
Of mud and slush, Dante assigned to the gluttons.

Chelone

Chelone was a nymph, transmogrified to a tortoise
Because she was late for the wedding of Zeus and Hera.
She'd dawdled along the lower slopes of Olympus,
And when she arrived, the party was all over.
The Father of Gods and Men was not amused,
And, as I said, he turned her into a tortoise.
The story's told in a Homeric Hymn,
And if like me you don't really read Greek,
You'll have to make do with Shelley's version of it.
Now it was Hermes, Zeus's son by Maia
Who reversed Chelone's doom. No sooner was Hermes born,
He left the cave where his mother had brought him forth.
He set out on his career – for he was to be
The god of travellers, heralds and of merchants,
And likewise of thieves, and of slick talkers
Lord of the standing stones. The first thing that he did
Was to purloin the prize cattle-herd belonging to his brother,
Apollo – lord of the sheep-fold and bright god of day –
And being a growing boy with a healthy appetite
The infant Hermes quickly consumed
All those prize beeves. And shortly after that
He found the tortoise, creeping along,
With her slow pace bearing her heavy load
A great curved shell, and eating buttercups no doubt
And asparagus shoots. Hermes knew who she was –
'Do not repine, Chelone. It's I will transform you;
And when I have done, you will be loved by all men,
And welcome at parties. You will be carried thither.
You shall order their dances with your music.
You shall accompany their joyful songs.'
With this he seized Chelone the poor tortoise,
And from her hollow shell he made a sounding lyre.
Scooping out her body, he strung her shell
With the taut strings of her guts. And when his brother
Finally tracked him down, he found him
Sitting among the cattle bones, having enjoyed his dinner,
Strumming his lyre, whose sounding strings
Echoed among the mountains. Then young Hermes
Confessed his fault and begged his brother's pardon,
And for a peace-offering, proffered his new-strung lyre.

Apollo accepted it. Henceforth
These two were friends and boon-companions – Apollo,
Patron of song, Hermes of eloquence.
So mark this, reader – if it's your vocation
To take the poet's role, it's necessary
You'll be transformed as slow Chelone was
Into a sounding instrument of song.
But mark this also, it shall be your doom
To have your guts torn out, your nerves drawn taut,
You to become simply a sounding shell –
Whether at festivals or in the market place
Or else among the echoing mountain solitudes.

The Clock Stopped

It's on a high shelf,
And I'm sure I always heard it.
Or someone must wind it.
Every hour, in fact, four knights came out,
And rode around, and jousted, and at the quarters
A bear-ward came, and a dancing bear –
They performed a gavotte together.
But not lately – silence now is just silence,
Or else a volley of phrases too loud to be heard
Where the knights, and the bear-ward and the dancing bear, and I
(Who think I heard them) are gathered up into a total silence,
Or else a music too loud for the listening.

Mushroom Universities

The mushroom and the toadstool, the agaric, the boletus,
Unsure of their own identities, have doubts where their allegiances lie –
Whether to the animal or the vegetable kingdoms.
The great Linnaeus, Erasmus Darwin tells us,
Had similar questions about these fungi.
This must be the reason why so many
Mushroom universities have sprung up,
The length and breadth of England.
They admit human beings as students also,
While the professors are half and half –
At least some of them.

Omar Khayyam

He wrote a treatise upon algebra,
The faceless numerals came to a masked ball,
Reformed the calendar, the feast-days and fast-days
Marched to the orders of the sun and moon.
He improvised verses over the wine cup –
Some, true believers, looked askance at this –
Others, lovers and tipplers, gathered them up,
And so, at English dining tables we recall them.

The World's My Oyster

'The world's my oyster,' I said
As all young men say, 'and I will bash it open
With my pen or sword.' But what I found inside
Was a blind, sensitive, limbless lamellibranch,
That cringed when lemon juice was squirted on it,
And also sweated one or two small pearls
From time to time, but that was when
It was feeling rather out of sorts.
Swallow oysters whole if you can get them
Or leave them to the shrill-voiced oyster-catcher
Saint Olaf's bird, that haunts the northern shores.

The Pompadour Chatterer

A French ship voyaging from the New World,
Its hold crammed with objects of value and natural curiosities,
Among the last a stuffed bird, designated
As a gift for Madame de Pompadour,
To wear in her high-piled wig —
But she never got it.
All such things were handed over
To the British Museum and duly catalogued —
The bird was named the *Pompadour Chatterer* —
The name it is still known by
In ornithological circles.

She never got it, that arrogant woman —
Jeanne Antoinette Poisson, Marquise de Pompadour,
Who had started her career
As the plain bourgeoise Madame Poisson,
The tilting of whose wig, the flirting of whose fan,
Could seal the fate of provinces and satraps —
And after that, the deluge.

An Ibis at Blackpool

A Bald-Faced Ibis, somewhat disoriented,
At the time of his autumn migration,
Finished up, not in West Africa, but Blackpool Sands,
Settled there, lonely and frustrated, hoping for a mate.
If this had happened in Victorian times
The Ibis doubtless had been shot
As a rarity and put in a glass-case,
Stuffed, as a centre-piece
For an over-furnished drawing-room –
Or else, his corpse
Would have been handed over to a taxonomist
To count the bones in his palate,
The muscles in his thigh –
Cousin of the curlew or sibling of the stork?
But now he's been placed in a wildlife park,
Caged in a nice clean pool,
With plenty of food,
And surrounded by mirrors, images of himself,
So he'll suppose he's among friends
And a mate may come –
We treat poets in much the same fashion.

To find the Sacred Ibis now you'd have to go
Beyond Upper Egypt, to the Sudan or Ethiopia –
For he is Hermes Trismegistus, Thoth,
Grand Secretary of the whole synod of Immortal Gods,
Inventor of the Hieroglyphic script,
Master of all wisdom.

The Glossy Ibis, on the other hand –
Purplish-black in hue, is, we are told.
A not infrequent visitor to Norfolk,
And eastern counties generally,
Though not to Liverpool or Lancashire, even so some maintain
The Glossy Ibis was the Liver-Bird.

'*In medio tutissimus ibis*' – you'll go safest by the middle way –
The motto of all good British ornithologists –
The Roman poet's counsel to each one of us
Who seeks to sail among the Clashing Rocks
Of disagreement and controversy.

A Tufted Duck

Of all the water-fowl the one I love the best
Is the little tufted duck. You can see them any day
In Kensington Gardens, on the Round Pond,
Along with the noble swans, the moorhens and the mallards.
Some years after the end of the war, I recall
(London was still littered with bomb-sites) a tufted duck
Reared her brood on one of them – just off the Charing Cross Road.
And when the time was ripe, she led them all
Down the busy street, across Trafalgar Square,
Then to the Thames, and introduced them
To that element, where they must make their living.
A policeman held the traffic up to let them pass along
The whole way. This, I think,
Could only have happened in England –
And I bless England for it.

The Nightingale's Ode to John Keats

It was round about breakfast time that you heard me –
In the garden of the Hampstead cottage you had rented –
Not in a forest, not by romantic moonlight
I sang as you do, to define my status,
And to attract a female. Now my brood is flown –
As for Miss Fanny Brawne – she went on waltzing
After you were gone – married a solid Jewish businessman.
She lies in Chelsea in her own bourgeois grave.
The doctor sent you to Italy – in the hold of a ship –
The other passengers all touched with the same disease.
You were buried in the town ditch, the Protestant cemetery
Near dozens of aristocratic young English tourists who
Died of malaria on the Grand Tour –
And much later on, Ronald Firbank,
Of all unlikely people! The authorities
Didn't know he was a Catholic.
We'll glance back again
At your Hampstead days. You needn't have been poor
If your uncle had managed sensibly your mother's bequest.
He wanted you to take a proper job
As an apothecary. You talked of 'calling out'
The hostile reviewers – this was gentlemen's talk and where
Was your tenderness for Nature when with a friend,
You walked across the Heath, taking potshots
At innocent tomtits? Stow it, Keats!

On Christmas Day

Oxen bellow; donkeys hee-haw; camels bubble;
Redbreast and Dicky Dunnock
Squabble for a few spilt crumbs – they are you and I,
Fellow parishioners, church-goers or not;
A new-born infant cries; the astrologers
Unroll their star-mats on the same stable floor,
But find no clue, not knowing
They have already arrived.
But for vigilant and untutored shepherds
Angelic hands unlock the counterpoint
That streams through a non-symmetric Cosmos.

Poem for Easter

A stone rolled away, a vacant tomb,
Linen clothes folded, the voice of a gardener
Who was not a gardener – women's tales,
And other rumours – a stranger on the road,
Texts expounded – a recognition
In the breaking of bread. And then
'I go a-fishing' – back
To the quotidian reality, the boring necessity
Of earning a living. A figure on the shore –
The miraculous draught again,
Every species of fish, and then
The recognition, the submission, the commission –
'Feed my sheep' – the renewal
Which every spring contains,
One with the eternal renewal
Of the all-embracing, illimitable cosmos of love.

St Godric of Finchale (1069–1170)

A pirate, before he became a hermit –
I'm glad of that first career of his –
(You know where you are with pirates,
But a merchant will always cheat you if he can)
Godric spent his retiring years composing hymns
To the Mother of God, the Star of the Sea,
In English too. But there wasn't much poetry about then
For all our betters seem to talk Norman French. It's true – at Senlac –
A jongleur rode in front of Duke William's host,
Singing 'The Song of Roland' – a new story to us –
And throwing his sword in the air and catching it
And as for Godric, I hope he'll look after us now
As we – didn't we? – tried to look after him

A Bit of a Tall Order

A bit of a tall order to ask from me
A positive and optimistic poem,
Who am the translator of Giacomo Leopardi
Whose *infinita vanita del tutto* was his final answer.
But I have to admit, each year before spring starts
A missal-thrush sings not far away
Each new morning and once I woke
To find a grey squirrel fooling about on my window-ledge.

Pandora's Box

To begin with, it wasn't a box, but an urn —
The Greeks were not very good at boxes,
A box full of troubles according to Hawthorne,
But when in curiosity Pandora opened it
They were dispersed through the waste of the world,
But Hope remained to console mankind. No, rather
To torment mankind with false expectation of blessings —
And it was the blessings that were dispersed and wasted
So Hesiod said and he was Homer's successor

Devizes

Devizes, in Wiltshire is chiefly remembered
For the young man, whose ears
Or some say, more intimate organs
Were of different sizes.
John Betjeman, I recall particularly disliked Devizes.
'As soon as I heard,' he once said,
'That boy scout in the Montagu case
'Came from Devizes, I knew he was lying.'
In the market place there's a notable statue –
A mediaeval baker's wife was charged
With selling false weight. Mediaeval laws
Of market inspection were extremely strict. She denied the charge –
Might she be struck dead,
She indignantly said – and immediately was,
So they erected a statue to this local heroine.
As a matter of fact, I don't think
I've ever visited, but just passed through
The town of Devizes. And of course I'm sure
That it is a totally charming place,
And all its boy scouts immaculately truthful.

In the Porcelain Factory

Once I was shown around a porcelain factory,
One of our best English producers of fine china
But what I remember best is a small man –
Hunchbacked he seemed or deformed in some way.
His only task to paint images of birds on cups or saucers.
This he did constantly and continually,
Not pausing to notice those of us who gazed at him.
I do not know if there was anyone to love him or to care for him.
His whole life this constant repetition
Of small images of love and song and freedom.
He must be gone now and who will remember him?

Edward Fitzgerald Meets Mother Goose
and Both Become Politically Committed

NOTE *I composed the following poems before breakfast, mostly in my bath. After I had set them down it occurred to me that they might be thought to have too little contemporary and social relevance. I have therefore prefaced each poem with a short note to show how ridiculous such a charge must be.*

Old Mother Hubbard

Effects of inadequate care for the elderly

Old Mother Hubbard, an impoverished crone
Went to her closet looking for a bone
To give her faithful dog. The shelves were bare –
So the unhappy quadruped had none.

Little Miss Muffet

Regrettable incidence of arachnophobic neurosis in the population at large

Miss Muffet sat on a rustic seat:
She had a bowl of curds and whey to eat.
There came a spider of prodigious size –
The maiden turned, and made a fast retreat.

Tom, Tom the Piper's Son

Years of political misrule have led inevitably to the development of a criminal underclass

Delinquent Tom, who was the piper's son,
Purloined a pig – a felon on the run.
Tom apprehended, was chastised. The pig
Went to the spit, to roast till it was done.

Little Bo Peep

Wasteful nature of unplanned animal husbandry

A shepherdess who lost her fleecy sheep;
She sat upon mossy bank to weep.
'Let them alone,' a kindly neighbour said
'And they'll return – but sans their tails, Bo-peep.'

The Queen of Hearts

Irresponsible behaviour of hereditary monarchy – a conflation of two sources

The queen of hearts, as I have heard men say,
Baked some jam tarts upon a summer's day.
The thieving knave came sneaking in her kitchen,
Observed the tarts, and stole them clean away.

'Such theft of royal assets isn't funny!'
The king cried out in wrath. 'Jam tarts cost money!'
While he retired to work out his next budget
The queen consoled herself with bread and honey,

A maid meanwhile, down in the garden close,
Was hanging garments up. Who would suppose
A blackbird, that had broken through a pie-crust
Swooping from skywards, should peck off her nose?

Jack Sprat and his Wife

Importance of maintaining a balanced diet

Scared of cholesterol, the aged Mr Sprat
On no account whatever would eat up fat.
His wife detested meat stringy and lean –
They left a well-licked platter for all that.

Baa Baa Black Sheep

Unfair distribution of natural resources in a class-ridden patriarchal society

You, bleating sheep, whose hue is deepest black,
Pray estimate the wool upon your back.
'The answer's yes and no – come shearing time
I'll bear three loads: each one will fill a sack.'

'Two bags my master certainly will claim,
And one is for his haughty wife, my dame.
But they'll spare none for the poor lad who weeps
Along the byways, in his rags and shame.'

Pussy's in the Well

Need for a responsible attitude to the natural world

Sound the alarm, ring the tocsin bell –
A cat is drowning in the village well.
Bold Johnny Stout shall save her. Johnny Green
It was who pushed her in, I grieve to tell.

Little Jack Horner

A confessional poem

Into his Christmas pie he thrust a thumb,
Extracting from it a delicious plum.
'How good and great am I,' Jack Horner said,
'Vastly superior to the vulgar scum.'